Twenty to **Stitch**

One-patch Quilts

Carolyn Forster

Search Press

First published in 2017

Search Press Limited
Wellwood, North Farm Road,
Tunbridge Wells, Kent TN2 3DR

Reprinted 2017

Text copyright © Carolyn Forster 2017

Photographs by Paul Bricknell at
Search Press Studios

Photographs and design copyright
© Search Press Ltd 2017

Print ISBN: 978-1-78221-376-5

Suppliers
If you have difficulty in obtaining any of the
materials and equipment mentioned in this
book, then please visit the Search Press
website for details of suppliers:
www.searchpress.com

Printed in China through Asia Pacific Offset

DEDICATION
*For anyone who wants to explore the infinite
possibilities of stitching one simple shape.*

Acknowledgements
*Thank you to Sizzix and their wonderful selection of
one-patch dies, and all the template manufacturers for
making the cutting out of one-patch quilts so much easier.*

Contents

Introduction

Patchwork quilts sewn from just one pattern piece can offer endless satisfaction from a design point of view, as well as being easy to cut and sew. To start with, there is the great ease of only ever having to cut one shape out.

All of the quilts in this book are made with one patch and have no other shape in the quilt. The designs they produce are often referred to as tessellating patterns, as the shapes connect to each other with no gaps in between.

One-patch quilts are great for the novice as well as the experienced sewer. One simple shape, such as a square, can simply be sewn as a 'happy scrappy' quilt, where the positioning of fabrics is random and the same fabric is used more than once. A more complicated shape such as the jewel, for example, is slightly more tricky to sew, but a whole range of design possibilities exist, all depending on your fabric selection.

One of the first documented single-patch quilts was a hexagon quilt in *Godey's Lady's Book*, published in 1835. This patch is still a favourite, but there are many others that offer design versatility. You will see in the following pages some of the ideas that these quilts can inspire. Each project includes the template at actual size and one or two ideas for putting your shapes together (although there are many more than we have space for!).

A one-patch quilt can be sewn as a charm quilt; this is when each piece of the quilt is stitched from a different piece of fabric. These quilts are often created over a long period of time while the fabrics are being collected. To speed up the process, people often exchange fabrics with fellow quilters or family members. Fabrics from old clothes can be used, as well as pieces swapped with friends and family, making them into a memory quilt.

The patches in the book come roughly in order of stitching difficulty, but don't let that influence your choice of patch – let your imagination and your fabrics take the lead. Make your patchwork as large or as small as time and fabrics allow, and refer to the Stitching know-how information on pages 46–48 for basic guidelines on joining, quilting and finishing.

Square

Instructions:

The simplest and most common of shapes can be sewn into an infinite number of designs. Inspiration can be taken from cross stitch designs and pixelated images.

To cut squares from fabric that include the seam allowance, any size you like, follow this simple formula: decide on the finished side size and add 5mm (¼in) for the seam allowance.

Stitching

The squares can be stitched in rows (see Option 1) or in unit blocks (see Option 2), depending on the design and method of working. Choose whichever you prefer.

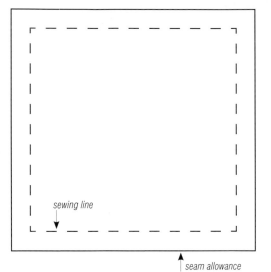

sewing line

seam allowance

How to join the shapes:

Option 1

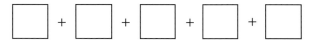

Option 2

Design idea 1

Design idea 2

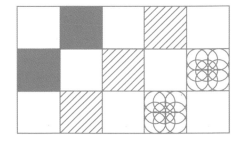

6

This pattern in this quilt follows Design idea 1, shown opposite.

Half-square Triangle

Instructions:

Triangles open up a whole new area of design ideas. Designs can be based on the play of light and dark within the square, or they can just be plain scrappy to use up what is at hand.

To cut half-square triangles from fabric at any size you want (that includes the seam allowance), follow this simple formula: decide what length the finished side of the square will be and add a 2.25cm ($^7/_8$in) seam allowance.

Stitching:

Sew the triangles together along the long bias edge to make squares first. Once these pieces are together, you can approach the stitching as you do with the squares on the previous page by working in rows or units.

How to join the shapes:

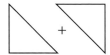 + =

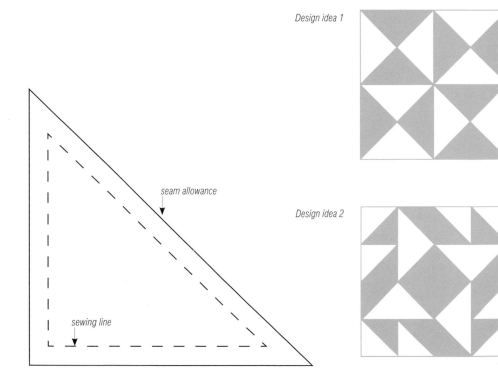

Design idea 1

Design idea 2

seam allowance

sewing line

The pattern in this quilt shows a different design option from the two opposite, using contrasting lights and darks to emphasise the triangles.

Quarter-square Triangle

Instructions:

Explore the design possibilities that a single unit of four triangles can make, or plan something larger depending on your time and fabric stash.

To cut fabric quarter-square triangles any size you like, follow the simple formula: decide on the length of the longest side and cut squares of fabric adding a 3cm (1¼in) seam allowance to the square. Then cut the square into four triangles.

Stitching:

Stitch the triangles into squares first, then proceed to stitch these either into rows or to work in units.

How to join the shapes:

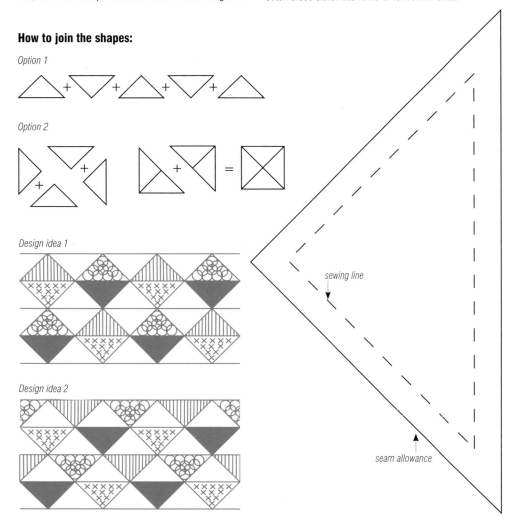

Option 1

Option 2

Design idea 1

Design idea 2

sewing line

seam allowance

The pattern in this quilt shows a different design option from the two opposite, giving a stacked triangle effect.

Rectangle Triangle

Instructions:

These rectangle triangles offer many subtle and interesting designs, taking things one stage further than the basic triangle. Play with individual design units, or plan something stunning on a design wall.

Stitching:

These can be approached in the same way as half-square triangles. Sew the pieces into rectangles first. Stitch the rectangles into rows or units to create your patchwork.

How to join the shapes:

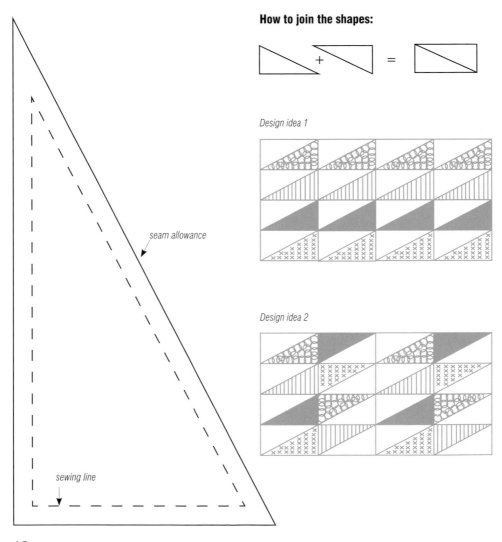

Design idea 1

Design idea 2

seam allowance

sewing line

This pattern in this quilt shows a lovely, almost undulating, movement of colour across the piece.

Rectangle

Instructions:

Rectangles can be used quickly and easily for the simplest of brick-type quilt designs and played with endlessly to form secondary designs including pinwheels, stripes and medallions.

Stitching:

These can be approached in the same way as squares. Stitch into rows or units to create your patchwork.

How to join the shapes:

Option 1

Option 2

Design idea 1

Design idea 2

seam allowance

sewing line

This pattern in this quilt follows Design idea 2, but with dark and light colours reversed for a different effect.

House or Prism

Instructions:

If you have not used this patch before, then you are in for a treat. Lined up in rows, it can look like streets of houses, yet transforms itself into a lovely abstract design unit when sewn in pinwheels of four.

Stitching:

If you are working on the design in rows, like a street of houses, stitch the rows first. Then set the rows in to each other (see page 46). The remaining side of the row will be straight and you can sew this in a line.

How to join the shapes:

Option 1

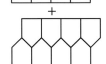

Option 2

Option 3

seam allowance

sewing line

Design idea 1

Design idea 2

The pattern in this quilt follows Design idea 1, shown opposite.

Tile or Double Prism

Instructions:

This patch makes a truly charming quilt and is great for using up fabric scraps. With some planning, you can create new shapes using some clever colour placement.

Stitching:

Stitch the patches together in rows, side by side, starting and stopping 5mm (¼in) from the raw edge. Then set these rows into each other, pivoting at each turn. It may seem fiddly to start with, but you will soon get the hang of it.

How to join the shapes:

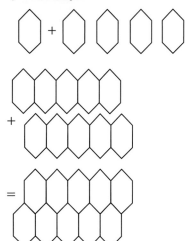

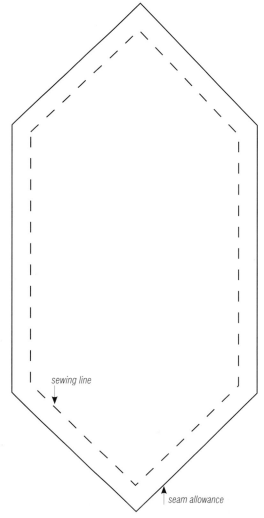

sewing line

seam allowance

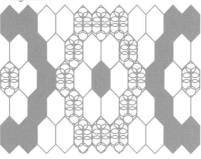

Design idea 1

Design idea 2

This pattern in this quilt is a random design on a blue theme.

45° Diamond

Instructions:

Lots of interesting patterns can be created with this simple diamond, but the stitching is usually very straightforward.

Stitching:

This patch is most easily stitched in straight lines of rows of patches. Flip the shape over to create designs with more movement, such as the zigzag in Design idea 1 below.

How to join the shapes:

Option 1

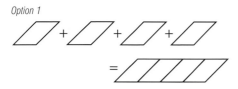

Option 2

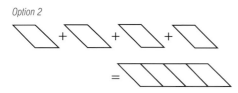

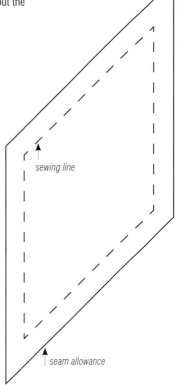

sewing line

seam allowance

Design idea 1

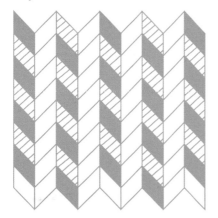

Design idea 2

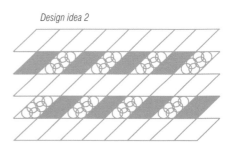

The pattern in this quilt follows an attractive zigzag across the piece.

60° Diamond

Instructions:

At first glance this is a similar patch to the 45° diamond, and the same type of designs can be created in lines as before. However, this diamond can also be stitched into stars and cubes, leading to whole new avenues of creativity.

Stitching:

These diamonds open up a whole new range of design possibilities starting with gentle zigzags and moving on to cubes, hexagons and stars. Use the fabrics to create 3-D effects in your quilt.

How to join the shapes:

Option 1

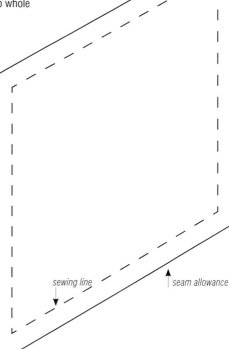

sewing line   *seam allowance*

Option 2

Option 3

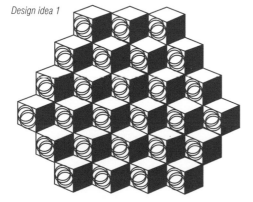
Design idea 1

 Design idea 2

The pattern in this quilt follows a different design idea from those shown opposite, creating lovely star shapes.

Kite

Instructions:

This is a shape that will become a firm favourite with you. The design possibilities open up before you, from triangles to hexagons.

Stitching:

You may find it easier to stitch your design into triangles first. It will be easier to set in the pieces in small units rather than when they become hexagons and may be more unwieldy, especially if you are using a sewing machine.

How to join the shapes:

Option 1

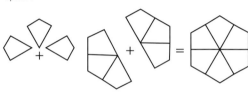

Option 2

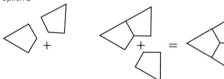

sewing line

seam allowance

Design idea 1

Design idea 2

These kites form hexagons in two different fabrics before being sewn together.

Equilateral Triangle

Instructions:

This is a lovely shape to play with; easily sewn into larger units such as diamonds, hexagons and larger triangles. On the other hand, it also lends itself beautifully to scrappy charm quilts easily sewn in comfortable rows.

Stitching:

Depending on your design, work in rows or smaller units before compiling the larger piece.

How to join the shapes:

Option 1

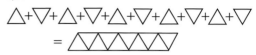

Option 2

Design idea 1

Design idea 2

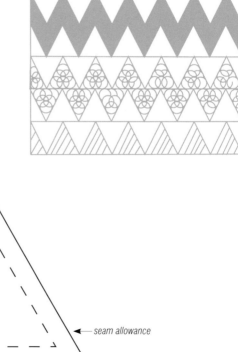

sewing line

seam allowance

26

The pattern in this quilt follows a different design from those shown opposite, creating light and dark diamond shapes.

Tumbler

Instructions:

This long, stretched version of the half-hexagon can give your designs a rather different feel. It's fun to get to grips with the different variations this patch can offer, and it's a great design for using up scrap fabric.

Stitching:

This patch is easily stitched in rows, omitting any need to set in pieces. You can achieve some very diverse patterns by choosing your fabrics carefully.

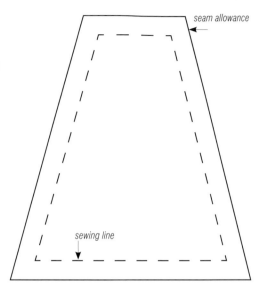

seam allowance

sewing line

How to join the shapes:

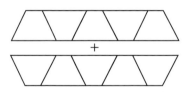

Design idea 1

Design idea 2

The pattern in this quilt follows Design idea 2, shown opposite.

Half-square

Instructions:

This is a great little shape that can make so many different quilts. When there is a stark contrast between the two patches in the square, many different combinations can be worked into quite different-looking designs.

Stitching:

Stitch the patches into squares before continuing to larger units or rows.

Design idea 1

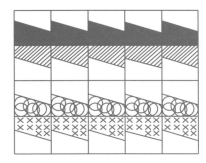

Design idea 2

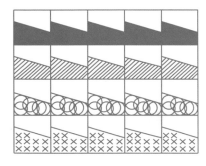

How to join the shapes:

Option 1

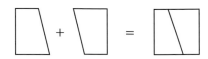

Option 2

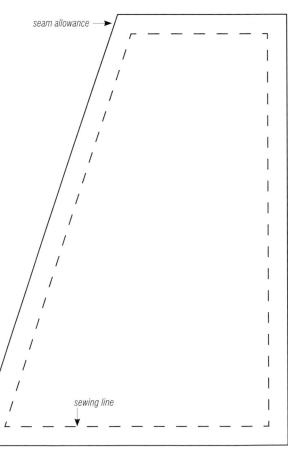

seam allowance ⟶

sewing line

The pattern in this quilt follows Design idea 1, shown opposite.

Half-hexagon

Instructions:

This is a really useful shape to use in your quilts. It allows you to stitch a hexagon quilt without any set-in piecing, as it can all be done in rows. This shape offers so much more, though, and it is well worth delving into your fabric stash to explore the possibilities.

Stitching:

Both options below show you how to work in rows, removing the need to set in any pieces.

How to join the shapes:

Option 1

Option 2

sewing line

seam allowance

Design idea 1

Design idea 2

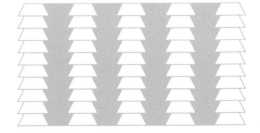

The pattern in this quilt follows a different design from those shown opposite, creating lovely hexagons shapes.

Braid

Instructions:

It is amazing how one shape can offer so many possible quilts, all of which look so different. Have fun using up your scraps in all the quilt possibilities this patch opens up to you.

Stitching:

The easiest way to stitch linear designs is in lines. This braid design is worked in lines and, once you get started, it all comes together easily.

How to join the shapes:

Option 1

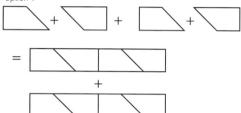

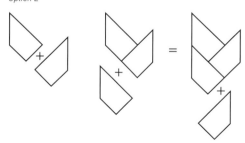

Option 2

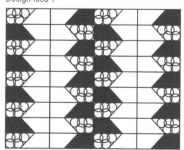

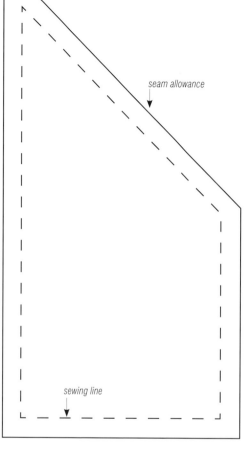

seam allowance

sewing line

Design idea 1

Design idea 2

The positioning of the fabric in this quilt has created an attractive stripy pattern with a red/pink theme.

Clam Shell

Instructions:

The question often asked of this pattern is which way up it goes – ultimately, it is up to the maker. Either way, it is worth having a go at this classic patch, especially to practise perfecting your curves.

Stitching:

I stitch this in diagonals, half a clam at a time (see right).

How to join the shapes:

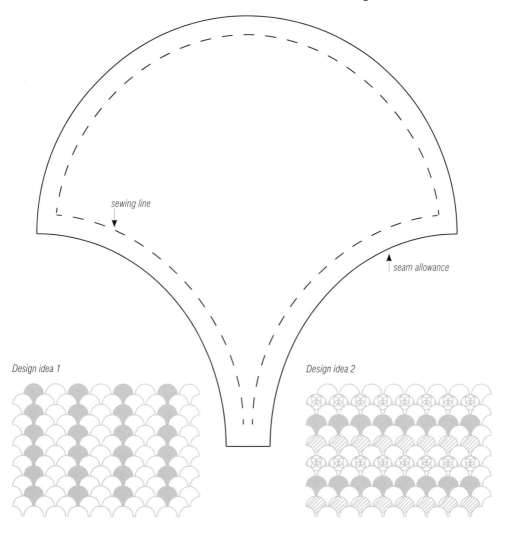

sewing line

seam allowance

Design idea 1

Design idea 2

The pattern in this quilt is completely random, giving it a homemade charm.

Jewel

Instructions:

Two quite different designs can be made from this patch. Both lend themselves to the use of scraps, but if time and inclination allow, some elaborate overall designs can be produced.

Stitching:

Stitch either design as the smaller units first, then set them in to each other to create the quilt.

How to join the shapes:

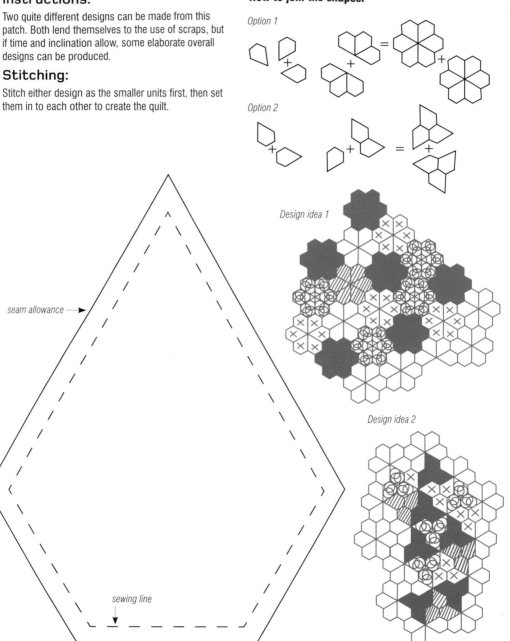

Option 1

Option 2

seam allowance ▶

sewing line

Design idea 1

Design idea 2

The pattern in this quilt follows Design idea 1, shown opposite, creating a pretty flower design.

Hexagon

Instructions:

This is the shape most people have in mind when thinking of one patch and tessellating patchwork. Most commonly worked in the EPP method (where you tack/baste around the shape – see page 47), but easily worked in the American piecing method, it cuts out the need to use papers and is then easily transferable to a sewing machine.

Stitching:

This is often worked in smaller units such as a Grandmother's Flower Garden pattern, then sewn into a larger unit.

How to join the shapes:

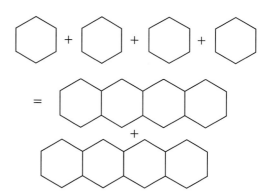

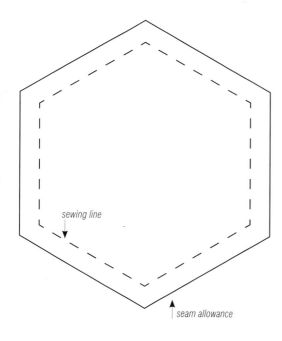

sewing line

seam allowance

Design idea 1

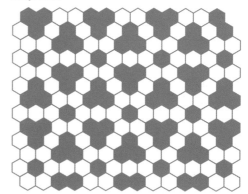

Design idea 2

The pattern in this quilt is made by creating dark, wavy lines separated by light ones, with a blue and beige theme.

Apple Core

Instructions:

A great shape for practising your curved piecing and, once you get the knack, this patch will hold no fear. If it seems a bit daunting, then practise using a larger template before attempting a smaller shape.

Stitching:

This is most easily worked in rows, or sew four patches together to make a square, then work these into rows.

How to join the shapes:

Option 1

Option 2

Design idea 1

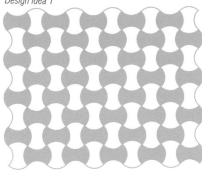

Design idea 2

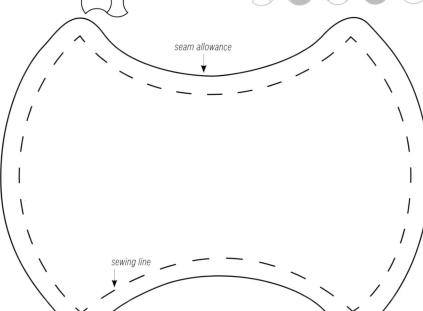

seam allowance

sewing line

The pattern in this quilt follows Design idea 1, shown opposite.

Sewing know-how

Fabric & Thread

Cotton dress-weight fabrics are the easiest to stitch with if you are just starting out. Scraps of old clothes will hold personal memories and are fun to include and use. Make sure you choose areas of fabric that are not worn out. Any fabric you use should be clean and pressed flat.

Stitch with a good-quality sewing thread using a colour that tones with your fabrics.

Cutting the patches

You can use the template shapes in this book as they are, or increase or reduce the size on a photocopier if you prefer to use a different size, but keep the seam allowance (SA) at 5mm (¼in).

The most important things to note are:

• All the templates include a 5mm (¼in) SA and also show the stitch line. If you want a template without a SA, draw along the inner dashed line (the stitch line) of the template diagram.

• If you are hand sewing and want to draw in the stitch line, draw around a template cut to the size of the stitch line; then, before cutting out the fabric, add on an additional 5mm (¼in) SA all around, by eye, giving you the full size.

• If you are confident sewing without the marked stitch line, simply draw and cut out the patches at the SA line, and then sew them together using your presser foot width to guide you as to the SA.

Make your templates from firm card or template plastic. Template plastic is easy to cut with scissors and very durable. Use a fine-line permanent marker pen to label the template and note any stitching lines. Clear template plastic acts as a great window template if you want to use a certain motif from a fabric, as you can see through it to position it correctly. If you are repeating a motif for fussy cutting you can add balance points so that you always match the motif accordingly.

If you are using card as your template, photocopy the template and then stick it to the card. Cut out along the printed line. A card template is fine, but will not be as accurate if you use it repeatedly, as the edges become soft after a while.

Rotary cutting

Some of the shapes can be cut using a rotary cutter, mat and ruler. You will not have to make a template, but you will need to measure the shape and cut accordingly from the fabric. Cut these with a SA.

Die-cutting machines

Lots of the one-patch designs in the book are popular shapes that many die-cutting machine companies produce. This is a great way to cut lots of patches accurately that include the SA. If you are thinking of using English Paper Piecing (EPP), also consider buying pre-cut papers, which come in lots of different sizes and multiple quantity packets.

Stitching the patches

Using a sewing machine

All the patches in the book can be sewn on a machine (with the exception of the Clam Shell on page 36), but you will need to pay special attention to stitching the set-in pieces or curved pieces. These patches do not need a sewing line, as you will be guided by the 5mm (¼in) piecing foot on the sewing machine; cut them with the SA included.

When sewing the patches on the machine, you will be sewing through the seam allowance, unless you are setting pieces in. As you stitch through the seam allowance there is no need to secure the thread at the end of each seam. If you want the stitches to be more secure, then reduce your stitch length slightly to make a tighter seam. If you are stitching multiple pieces, then you can 'chain piece' by feeding the next set of patches under the foot as the last ones come out at the back. This saves thread and time.

Most patchwork pieces can be sewn in straight lines, but some require you to sew around a corner. This is known as a set-in seam or a 'Y' seam. For this to happen smoothly, you need to stop stitching where the 5mm (¼in) seam allowances intersect on the first seam of the 'Y'. Stop at this point and leave a tail of thread about 2.5cm (1in) long. This seam is then pressed open, thus allowing you to sew in the third patchwork piece. By not sewing through the seam allowance here and pressing the seam open, you are able to stitch and pivot at the intersection, allowing you to sew round the corner smoothly and neatly.

Sewing by hand with running stitch

If you have cut patches that include the SA, remember to mark in the stitching line if you don't feel experienced enough to judge by eye. (If you stitch the patches on the machine, then the foot guide will give you the correct SA.)

All the patches in the book can be sewn by hand using this method. Depending on how you have cut the patches, this will then guide you as to how you stitch them together. Thread the needle with toning thread no longer than the length of your arm. Start stitching with a knot and a backstitch and continue with a running stitch. Every inch or so make a backstitch to help keep a good tension. When you reach the end of the sewing line, make two or three backstitches to finish. Cut the thread, leaving a tail about 1.3cm (½in) long.

Patches with sewing line already drawn

These patches will be stitched together in the same way as the ones below, but the pinning is slightly different.

As you have lines on each patch, it is these that you need to match up rather than the raw edges. Place two patches with rights sides together with a pin going through the SA stopping point. Pin it into the other patch at the same point, and pin into the SA. Do the same at the other end, and when that is in place, use a couple of pins to match up the line between the two points, depending on the length of your seam.

Patches with no sewing line

These patches have the SA included, but no line to follow. If you are experienced then you will be able to stitch them together by eyeballing the sewing line. If you are not at that stage yet, then use a propelling pencil on the wrong side of the fabric to draw the line. Use a rotary cutting ruler or a Quilter's Quarter Marker™ to mark the line. You only need the line on the patch that will face you when you stitch.

Sewing by hand with papers

Also known as English Paper Piecing (EPP), this is perhaps the method most associated with one-patch or mosaic-style quilts. It is very precise and works well for some of the more intricate shapes that require set-in piecing. It is, however, more time-consuming due to the extra step of stitching or gluing the papers onto the fabric. Cut papers the finished size of the patches. Fabric patches should be cut larger by 5mm (¼in) or 1cm (³⁄₈in).

Place the paper on the wrong side of the fabric with a SA all round each side. Fold the fabric to the paper and tack/baste through all of the layers to keep the fabric in place, starting with a knot and finishing with a backstitch.

When the patches are ready, sew with right sides together using toning thread and an oversewing stitch to secure the edges together. When the design is complete, remove the tacking/basting from the patches and take the papers out.

Note:

Each design in the book is suitable for hand sewing, machine sewing and EPP. Some designs need to have set-in seams; these are the house (or prism), clam shell, jewel and hexagon (pages 16, 36, 38 and 42).

How big should I make my template?

You can use the templates the size they are in the book, or enlarge them using a photocopier. If you are planning to make a large bed quilt and have lots of small pieces of fabric to use up, don't make the template too large to use with the fabric (unless you want to piece it together first). However, a small template for a large project will mean it will take longer to stitch. With this in mind, if your finished quilt is going to be quite large, increase the size of the template so you get a good size that won't take too long to stitch. However, if you decide to adjust the size of your template, remember that the SA needs to stay at 5mm (¼in).

Bear in mind the scale and proportion of the design on the fabrics, too. If you have a large-scale print, then you might want to show this off with a larger template. If you like working with smaller patches, consider working on a smaller project such as a mini-quilt or a pillow cover. It would even be possible to make a small block/quilt of each of the one-patch templates and sew them all together with sashing – sampler style – into one big quilt.

How much fabric will I need?

One-patch designs lend themselves to scrappy-style quilts or charm quilts. Quilt instructions for such designs do not usually come with fabric quantity guidelines. As I am providing ideas for quilts in this book, rather than instructions on making specific quilts, there are no fabric quantities given, as there are too many variables, for example: How big is my template? How big do I want my finished quilt to be?

Some guidelines will help you to calculate how much fabric you need for a particular project. The way I work is as follows:

1 Find out how many templates you can cut from a fat quarter of fabric. Next, count how many templates fit across the width and then the length of the quilt. Multiply these together for the total number.

2 Divide this total number by the number of templates in a fat quarter. This number rounded up to a whole number will be the number of fat quarters you need.

This is just one way of working, so feel free to adapt it to your own methods.

Design options

There are so many ways to arrange these tessellating shapes that it would be almost impossible to describe them all. They may make different grids, or the grid may stay the same.

Doodle on paper or print off downloadable grids from the internet to experiment with what is possible. Colour these in using a pencil or use coloured pens, depending on your working preference, so that you can see the patterns clearly, and you will begin to get an idea of the wide range of options that exist before you begin to stitch.

There are numerous variations for each of the templates in this book so, although there are just twenty shapes to start you off, there are so many more different quilt variations you could sew.

Completing a quilt

Once the patchwork is complete, press it flat. Neaten up the edges by cutting them straight with scissors or a rotary cutter. If you want to keep any uneven edges that impart character to your quilt, you can appliqué the edges to a wide border on each side. This has the added advantage of making it larger without too much more work.

Layering and tacking/basting

Layer the patchwork onto wadding/batting and a backing fabric. Remember these should be larger than your patchwork top. Tack/baste the layers with tacking/basting stitches, spray baste glue or safety pins. The tacking/basting and pins will all be removed during the quilting process.

Quilting

The design you choose will also depend on your chosen method, but vermicelli, cross hatching, 45°, 60°, outline quilting, Amish wave and tying are all possible options if you do not want to outline quilt every patch.

Binding

Apply a sturdy binding to the quilt edges to finish it off. Cut the fabric strip 6.35cm (2½in) wide on the straight or bias. This continuous strip may need joins; make these on the bias to distribute the bulk of the join. Then fold the strip in half along its length, wrong sides together, and press flat. You can then bind the quilt using mitred corners or square corners. Sew by hand or machine stitch.